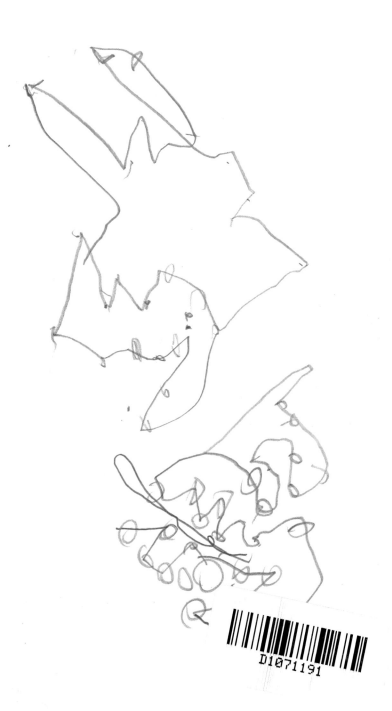

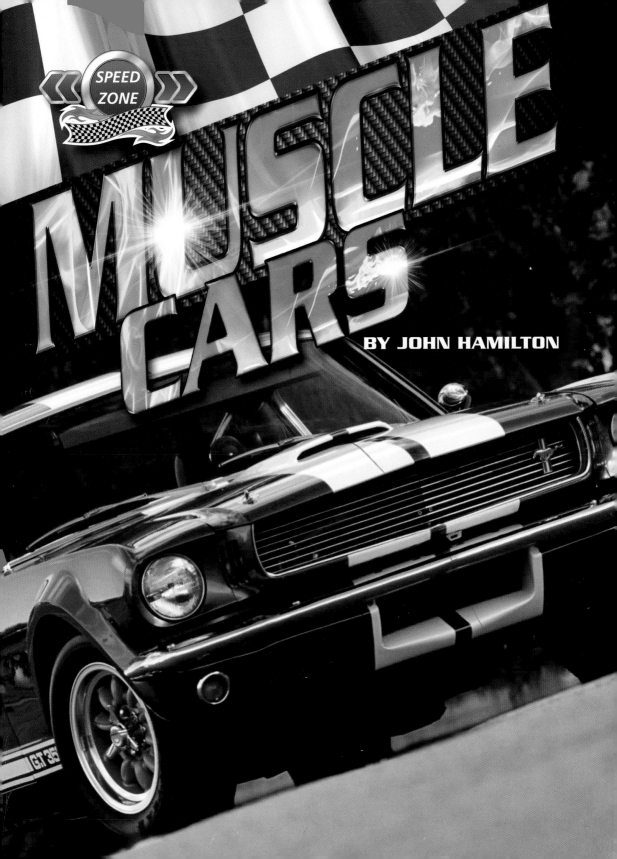

MUSCLE CARS

BY JOHN HAMILTON

VISIT US AT
WWW.ABDOPUBLISHING.COM

Printed in the United States of America, North Mankato, Minnesota.
062012
092012

 PRINTED ON RECYCLED PAPER

Editor: Sue Hamilton
Graphic Design: Sue Hamilton
Cover Design: John Hamilton
Cover Photo: Corbis
Interior Photos: Alamy-pgs 2-3, 14-15 & 32; Corbis-pgs 1, 6-13, 16-19, 21-25 & 28; General Motors-pgs 20, 27, 29 (bottom) & 30-31; Getty Images-pgs 26 & 29 (top); iStockphoto-pgs 4-5; Thinkstock-pg 1 (Speed Zone graphic).

ABDO Booklinks
Web sites about racing vehicles are featured on our Book Links pages. These links are routinely monitored and updated to provide the most current information available. Web site: www.abdopublishing.com

Library of Congress Cataloging-in-Publication Data

Hamilton, John, 1959-
  Muscle cars / John Hamilton.
     p. cm. -- (Speed zone)
  Audience: 8-15
  Includes index.
  ISBN 978-1-61783-529-2
  1. Hot rods--Juvenile literature. 2. Automobiles--Customizing--Juvenile literature. I. Title.
  TL236.3.H33 2013
  629.222--dc23
                          2012011951

CONTENTS

1970 Plymouth Superbird 440

MUSCLE CARS

Classic muscle cars are powerful, loud, ill-mannered, and always fun to drive.

1967 Pontiac GTO

These American-made high-performance vehicles were made for burning rubber and speeding down straightaways. Prized by collectors, muscle cars give bragging rights to any car buff lucky enough to own one of these beastly machines.

WHAT IS A MUSCLE CAR?

Some people think any fast, powerful car is a muscle car. But car buffs use certain guidelines. Muscle cars are usually American-made midsize cars from the 1960s and early 1970s. They are rear-wheel drive. They have powerful eight-cylinder engines that generate a lot of horsepower. Muscle cars are built for high performance and straight-line racing. However, they are also affordable family-style cars that can carry four or more passengers.

A customized 1973 Chevrolet Camaro Z28

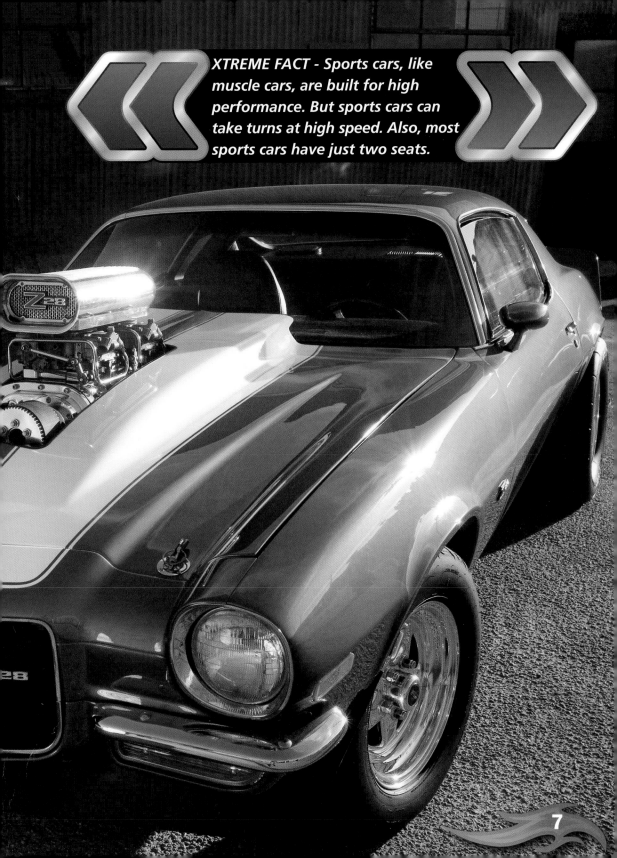

XTREME FACT - *Sports cars, like muscle cars, are built for high performance. But sports cars can take turns at high speed. Also, most sports cars have just two seats.*

By the 1950s, stock car racing and drag racing were becoming very popular. This "car culture" quickly spread. Regular people wanted their own fast and powerful cars. In 1949, Oldsmobile released the Rocket 88. It was a midsize car with a full-size V8 engine that produced 135 horsepower. It won many races.

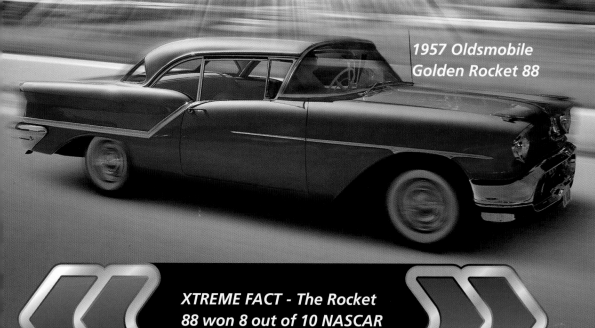

1957 Oldsmobile Golden Rocket 88

XTREME FACT - The Rocket 88 won 8 out of 10 NASCAR races in the 1950 season.

1955 Chrysler C-300

The stylish 1955 Chrysler C-300 had a gigantic 300-horsepower engine. It was a race winner, but many consider it too big and expensive to be a true muscle car. Even so, the public demanded more of these kinds of powerful cars.

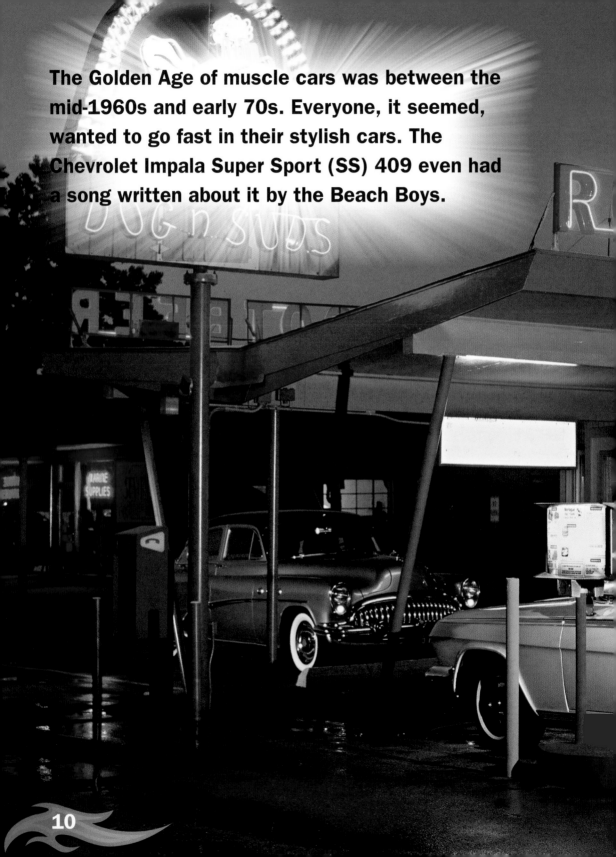

The Golden Age of muscle cars was between the mid-1960s and early 70s. Everyone, it seemed, wanted to go fast in their stylish cars. The Chevrolet Impala Super Sport (SS) 409 even had a song written about it by the Beach Boys.

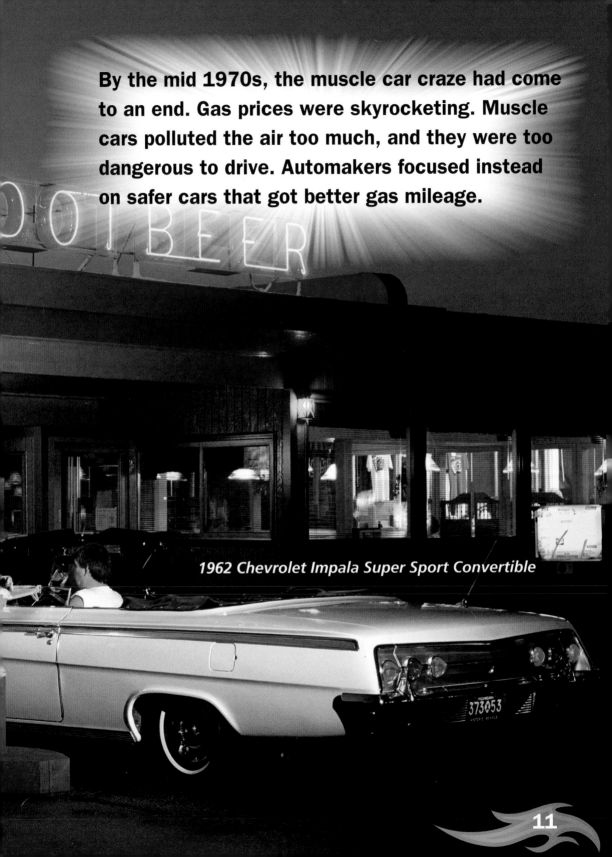

By the mid 1970s, the muscle car craze had come to an end. Gas prices were skyrocketing. Muscle cars polluted the air too much, and they were too dangerous to drive. Automakers focused instead on safer cars that got better gas mileage.

1962 Chevrolet Impala Super Sport Convertible

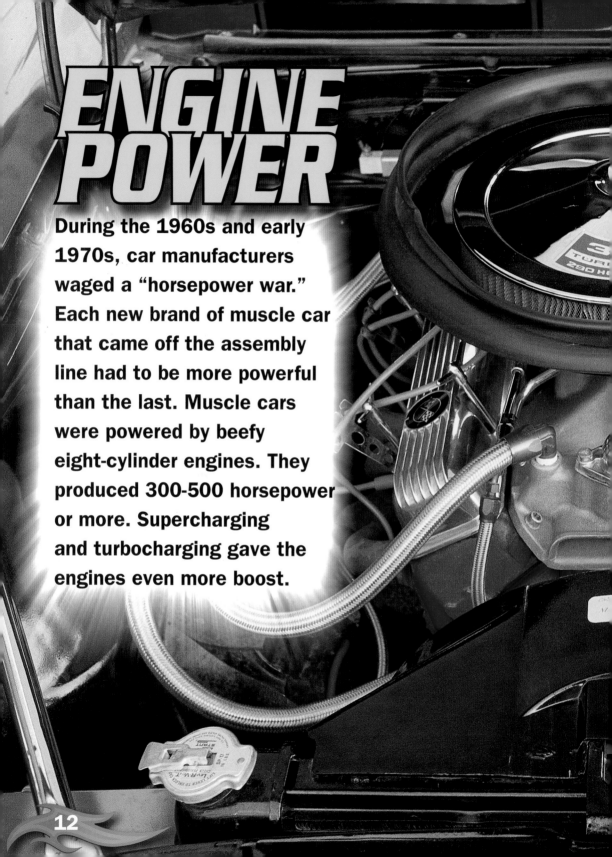

ENGINE POWER

During the 1960s and early 1970s, car manufacturers waged a "horsepower war." Each new brand of muscle car that came off the assembly line had to be more powerful than the last. Muscle cars were powered by beefy eight-cylinder engines. They produced 300-500 horsepower or more. Supercharging and turbocharging gave the engines even more boost.

The engine of a 1968 Chevrolet Camaro Z28.

XTREME FACT - Supercharging and turbocharging forces more air into an engine's cylinders, making it even more powerful.

CUSTOMIZING

Part of the fun of owning and collecting classic muscle cars is restoring their paint jobs and customizing parts.

Chevrolet Camaro SS

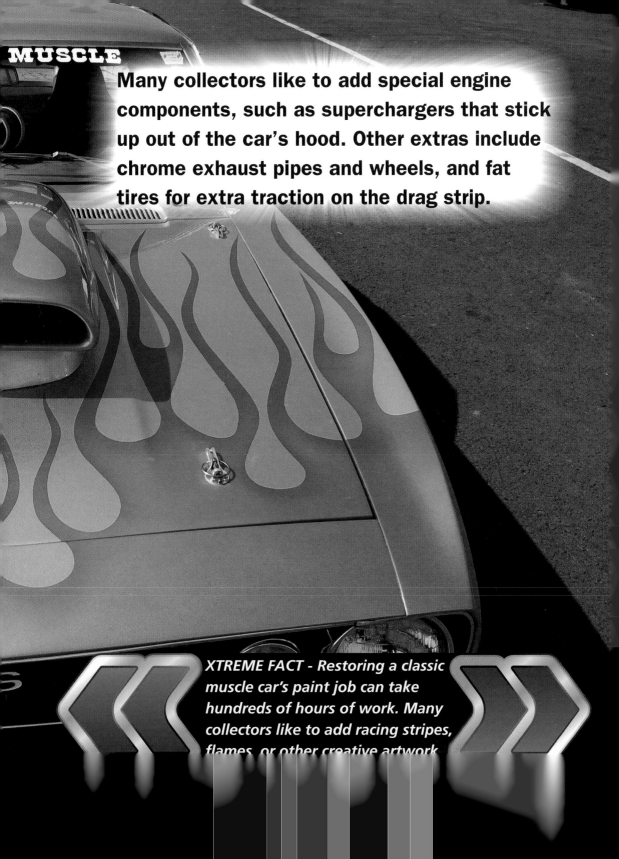

Many collectors like to add special engine components, such as superchargers that stick up out of the car's hood. Other extras include chrome exhaust pipes and wheels, and fat tires for extra traction on the drag strip.

XTREME FACT - Restoring a classic muscle car's paint job can take hundreds of hours of work. Many collectors like to add racing stripes, flames, or other creative artwork

PONTIAC GTO

Some say the 1964 Pontiac GTO was the first "true" muscle car. Pontiac engineers John DeLorean, Russell Gee, and Bill Collins installed a beefed-up 325-horsepower V8 engine into a midsize sedan. The result was an affordable beast of a car that became known affectionately as the "Goat" by muscle car lovers.

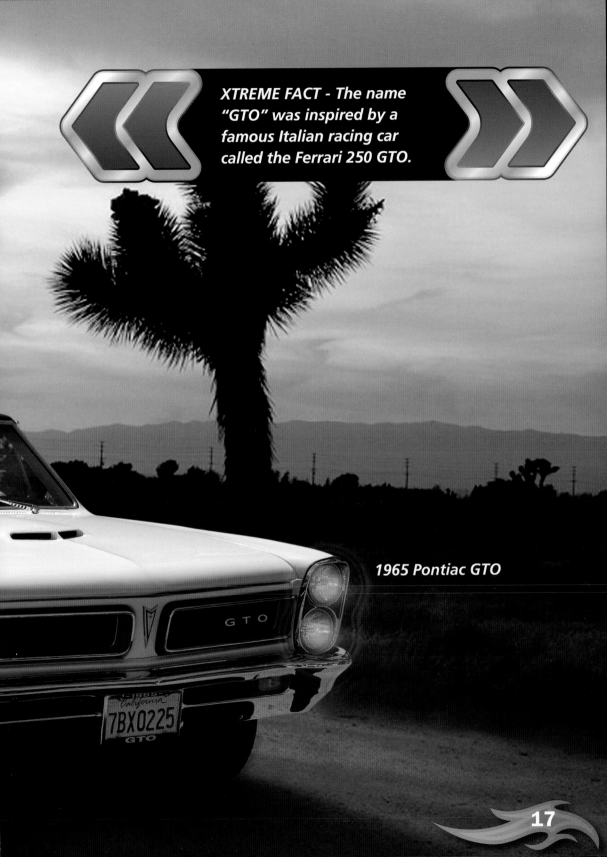

XTREME FACT - The name "GTO" was inspired by a famous Italian racing car called the Ferrari 250 GTO.

1965 Pontiac GTO

FORD MUSTANG

In the early 1960s, General Manager Lee Iacocca of Ford spearheaded the development of the Ford Mustang. The first models were affordable and stylish, but underpowered.

1968 1/2 (April)
Ford Mustang
428 Cobra Jet

Then Ford released one of the greatest, meanest muscle cars of all time, the 1968 Mustang 428 Cobra Jet. Its V8 engine was officially rated at 335 horsepower, but it was rumored to actually output closer to a tire-burning 410 horsepower.

XTREME FACT - Ford's rivals were quick to build cars that could compete against the Mustang. Examples of these "pony cars" included the Dodge Challenger and Chevrolet Camaro.

CHEVROLET CHEVELLE SS

The Chevelle was one of Chevrolet's first muscle cars, first released in the 1964 model year. In 1970, the Chevelle SS was let out of its cage. Its 450-horsepower V8 propelled the car from 0 to 100 miles per hour (161 kph) in just 13.3 seconds.

1970 Chevelle SS

PLYMOUTH HEMI 'CUDA

The rare 1971 Hemi 'Cuda was based on the Plymouth Barracuda. With its 425-horsepower V8 engine, it hunted down most of its pony-car competition and ate them for lunch.

1971 Plymouth Hemi 'Cuda

CHEVROLET CAMERO

Built low, wide, and fast, the Chevrolet Camaro was one of the most popular pony cars. The 1969 Camaro Z28 had an engine that was officially rated at 290 horsepower, but it was actually much more powerful. It also had a great suspension and braking package, making the Camaro a very well-rounded muscle car for cruising or racing.

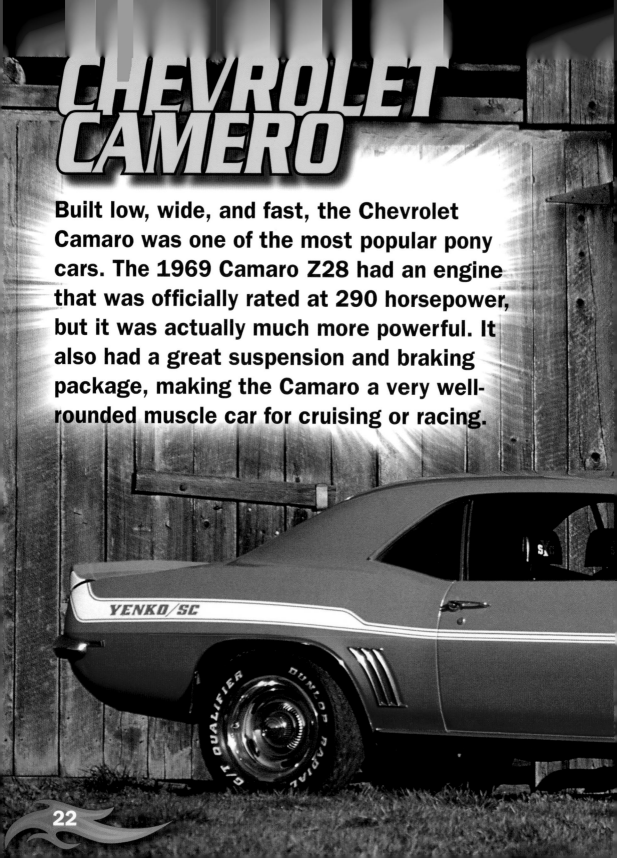

YENKO/SC

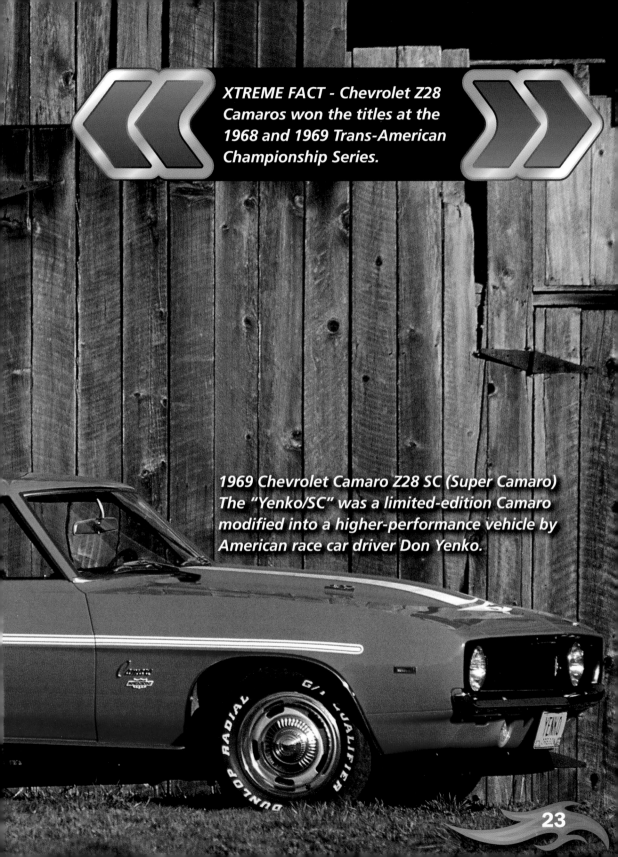

XTREME FACT - Chevrolet Z28 Camaros won the titles at the 1968 and 1969 Trans-American Championship Series.

1969 Chevrolet Camaro Z28 SC (Super Camaro) The "Yenko/SC" was a limited-edition Camaro modified into a higher-performance vehicle by American race car driver Don Yenko.

PLYMOUTH ROAD RUNNER

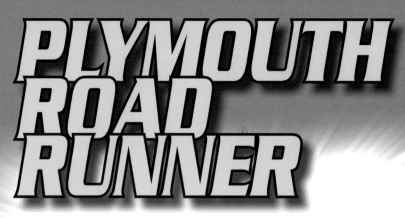

In 1968, Plymouth introduced the Road Runner. It had a name inspired by the Loony Tunes character (its horn even went "beep beep"), but it came with an optional 425-horsepower brute of an engine. The Road Runner was an economical, no-frills muscle car that was very popular.

1970 Plymouth Hemi Road Runner

AMERICAN MOTORS AMX

Even though the American Motors AMX is a two-seater, it is still considered a muscle car. Its design was based on the Javelin, a successful American Motors pony car. Many people were attracted to the AMX's long hood and Corvette-like performance.

1969 American Motors AMX

DODGE CHARGER R/T

The 1969 Dodge Charger R/T (the R/T stands for "Road/Track") was a high-performance package of the standard Charger. Besides a monstrous 425-horsepower hemi V8 engine, the Charger R/T had a distinctive curvy body and a famous hidden headlight grille. An orange Charger was nicknamed the "General Lee" on the TV show *The Dukes of Hazzard*.

Dodge Charger

PONTIAC FIREBIRD TRANS AM

The 1974 Pontiac Firebird Trans Am was one of the last classic muscle cars to be produced. It had a Super Duty engine that unofficially produced about 400 horsepower. Besides its sleek look, the Firebird Trans Am even had a painted firebird image that covered nearly the entire hood.

1976 Firebird Trans Am

MODERN MUSCLE CARS

Muscle cars are back with a vengeance. Today's powerful high-performance cars are faster, have better handling, and even get better gas mileage. Fuel-injected turbocharged engines, all-wheel drive, and traction control are common features.

The Ford 2013 Mustang Shelby GT500, with its mind-boggling 650-horsepower engine, would blow any classic muscle car out of the water.

While modern vehicles win in the performance department, fans of classic muscle cars will always smile fondly at the styling of their beloved street beasts, and the rumbling, high-octane thrill rides they delivered.

2011 Dodge Charger

Other modern muscle cars include new versions of the Dodge Charger (above) and Chevrolet Camaro (below).

2012 Chevrolet Camaro

GLOSSARY

Cylinder

A hollow chamber inside an engine where air and gasoline vapor mix. When ignited by a spark plug, the air/gas mixture explodes, forcing a metal piston inside the cylinder downward. The motion of the piston turns the gears that make the car move. Most classic muscle cars had eight cylinders working together to power the car. They were arranged in two rows in the shape of the letter "V," which is why these engines are referred to as V8s.

Fuel Injection

A system that mixes air and a fine spray of gasoline into an engine cylinder. Instead of using suction to draw in the gasoline, like a carburetor, fuel injection uses a small nozzle to spray gas under pressure directly into the cylinder. Fuel injection has been widely used on production automobiles for more than 30 years. It is generally more efficient than a carburetor, and saves gas.

Hemi

A hemi engine is one in which the roof of each cylinder's combustion chamber is shaped like a half-sphere (a *hemisphere*). Hemi engines have a better flow of air and fuel mixture through the cylinder, which can result in more efficiency and power.

Horsepower

Horsepower is a unit of measure of power. The term was originally invented to compare the power output of a steam engine with that of an average draft horse.

Supercharge

A supercharger compresses air and forces it into the combustion chambers, or engine cylinders. (The process is called forced air induction.) With this extra oxygen, more fuel can be added, which creates a bigger explosion in the chamber and gives the engine more power than it would have normally.

Turbocharge

Turbochargers use the power of exhaust gasses to power a compressor that injects additional air into the engine cylinders. Turbochargers are usually more efficient than superchargers.

Chevelle SS 454

INDEX

Ford Torino Cobra